The Ultimate Bubble Book

SOAPY SCIENCE FUN

by Shar Levine & Leslie Johnstone

Sterling Publishing Co., Inc.
New York

*For my children, Shira and Joshua, who finally made it to university, and for all the people who helped them get there: Dr. Linda Siegel, Andrew Kay, John Sund, Don Wilson, Bill Shaw, and of course, the amazing LJ and her chemistry magic.—**Shar***

*For Chris, Nick, and Megan and their dad, Mark!—**Leslie***

Thanks to C2 and Janice (Mom) for the edible bubbles. A very long time ago, when Shar owned Einstein's Science Centre, in Vancouver, BC, Canada, she had a dedicated young staff who used to teach a class on bubbles. They've now grown up and some even have children of their own. They all have real day jobs, too. Thanks to Alison Grafton, Sarah Hamblin, Sarah Anderson, Paxton Brewer, and the rest of the gang who used to play with Shar.

A big thanks also to Jim Becker at Cheesemouse for his explanation of the holes in Swiss cheese. As always, thanks to the kind folks at the Vancouver Public Aquarium for coming to our rescue with cool whale facts.

Edited by Nancy E. Sherman

Library of Congress Cataloging-in-Publication Data available

10 9 8 7 6 5 4 3 2 1

Published by Sterling Publishing Co., Inc.
387 Park Avenue South, New York, NY 10016
© 2003 by Shar Levine and Leslie Johnstone
Distributed in Canada by Sterling Publishing
c/o Canadian Manda Group, One Atlantic Avenue, Suite 105
Toronto, Ontario, Canada M6K 3E7
Distributed in Great Britain and Europe by Chris Lloyd at Orca Book
Services, Stanley House, Fleets Lane, Poole BH15 3AJ, England
Distributed in Australia by Capricorn Link (Australia) Pty. Ltd.
P.O. Box 704, Windsor, NSW 2756, Australia

Sterling ISBN 1-4027-0042-3

Contents

INTRODUCTION

There's something about bubbles that makes you smile. Perhaps it's the rainbow colors shining on the surface of these floating spheres. Maybe it's the challenge of making the biggest, longest-lasting bubbles that anyone has ever seen. It could be the joy of chasing after them to pop them with your finger. Whatever you like best about bubbles, this is the book for you.

It may be hard to believe that bubbles have anything to do with science. What may be even harder to believe is how much bubbles can teach you about the basic principles of surface tension, films, and math. Learning how bubbles form will help you make bubbles that don't burst so quickly, or at least predict when they will pop. So get ready to have some good clean fun with magic bubble mixtures.

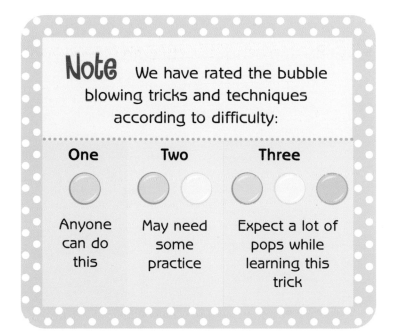

Note We have rated the bubble blowing tricks and techniques according to difficulty:

One	Two	Three
Anyone can do this	May need some practice	Expect a lot of pops while learning this trick

Note to Parents & Teachers

Despite the dire warnings to follow, as far as science experiments, you can't get much safer than those involving bubbles. You won't need any special equipment or hard-to-get supplies. The activities are safe for kids of all ages. Even small children can create huge bubbles with very little effort. The main concern here is to find a good place for bubble blowing. If you're making bubbles indoors, you'll need some absorbent material on the floor to prevent slips. You'll also need a good supply of cloth or paper towels to clean up spills and gooey solution. The best place for bubbles is outdoors, preferably out of the sun. Bubble solution can sting when it gets in your eyes. Have a clean washcloth and warm water handy for rinsing any burst bubbles that come in contact with eyes.

Cleanup

When you're finished making bubbles for the day, use paper towels to wipe up as much of the bubble solution as you can from tables and floors. Don't use water to clean up the leftover solution, as you'll merely make a foamy mess. Instead, sprinkle on a little white vinegar and cleanup will be a snap! The vinegar breaks down the bubble solution so it stops foaming.

Safety First

Bubble solutions contain liquid soaps. While these soaps won't cause blindness, they may sting when they come in contact with your eyes. If you have really sensitive skin, you might want to test the bubble solutions on a small patch of skin. If you break out in a rash, don't play with the bubbles.

Read through all of the instructions for an experiment before you begin.

Here are some other things you need to know.

Do's

1. Have a cloth and clean, warm water handy for unexpected bubble bursts. Wash out or rinse your eyes well if solution comes in contact with them.

2. Wear swimming goggles to protect sensitive eyes from exposure to burst bubbles.

3. Ask an adult before handling any materials or equipment.

4. Have an adult handle all sharp objects, such as knives or scissors.

5. After making bubbles, your hands are clean. But rinse your hands with warm water after handling bubble solution anyway, especially if you are going to eat.

6. Tell an adult immediately if you hurt yourself in any way.

7. Clean up the area where you have been using bubbles. The solution could cause others to slip and fall.

8. Keep the bubble solution away from small children and pets.

9. Label your container and safely store your bubble solution where it will not spill.

10. If you are blowing bubbles outdoors, make sure you wear proper protection from the sun.

11. Take off any jewelry, watches, or other accessories. Not only can they interfere with bubble blowing, they may get damaged.

12. Tie back long hair and roll up your sleeves or wear short-sleeved clothing when playing with bubbles.

Don'ts

1. Do not taste, eat, or drink any of the solutions.

2. Don't rub your eyes or touch your face if your hands have been in bubble solution.

3. Don't blow bubbles indoors without first getting an adult's permission. Bubbles can damage computers, artwork, delicate electronic equipment, and some curtains, carpets, and furniture fabric.

4. Try not to blow bubbles close to flower gardens as too much solution can harm plants and flowers.

5. Large quantities of bubble solution can kill or damage lawns.

6. At all times, keep bubble solution away from bodies of water where fish live and wildlife drink. Do not dump your used bubble solution in ponds, lakes, or rivers.

7. Keep solution away from public fountains. It may look funny to see a fountain overflowing with suds, but it's illegal and it's harmful to the environment—the police may want to have a long discussion with you.

Bubble Science & Bubble Solutions

The Science of Bubbles

You probably associate science experiments with things like test tubes and beakers. But there's complicated science at work even when you blow a bubble. The simple bubbles you blow involve the chemistry of the bubble solution, the physics behind all those wonderful colors, and the geometry defining the shape of the bubbles. In performing the experiments we describe, you will witness some of this science firsthand.

Three Basic Kinds of Bubbles

There are three basic kinds of bubbles:

1.
There are bubbles that form in water and float to the surface, then pop. These are the bubbles you see rising when a swimmer exhales under water.

2.
A second kind is formed when a bubble in a liquid floats to the surface and remains trapped there. This occurs when you blow bubbles into a glass of milk. The milk bubble is slower to pop than one in water. You can also see these bubbles when you beat an egg white. Look closely and you will see tiny bubbles in the liquid; it is these trapped bubbles that make beaten egg whites (and whipped cream) fluffy.

3.
The third kind is a floating bubble, one that is completely surrounded by a liquid film. This is the kind of bubble made with bubble solution and a wand. These bubbles float off into the air.

The Science of Soap

Bubbles can be made from many different materials, including glass, plastic, and egg whites, but here you will be using soap. There are all kinds of soaps and detergents. Soaps are the product of fats or oils heated together with water and lye, to which salt is added. Soaps differ depending on the fats or oils used to make them; some of them contain detergent. Detergents come from dinosaurs…well, indirectly they do. Detergents are made from petrochemicals found deep in the earth in deposits of fossilized plants and animals from the time of the dinosaurs. Detergent is used to change certain properties of water, making it behave differently and do things it doesn't otherwise do. Water is made up of particles called molecules. These molecules tend to stick to each other, giving water a property called surface tension. To see what this does, fill a drinking glass to the very top with water. Look at the top of the water and you will see a slight dome. Surface tension causes the water to form this dome; add soap or detergent and the water will sheet, or become a film. With the addition of soap or detergent, the water molecules assume a flat, thin arrangement, or pattern. The soap or detergent in bubble solution makes it have less surface tension, so better bubbles form when air is blown through it. If you have too much water in the mixture, it's hard to make bubbles form. If there is too little water, the bubbles tend to pop. Adding glycerin to the bubble solution helps keep the water in it longer; it slows down water's evaporation, or drying out.

Preparing Bubble Solution

Building a Better Bubble

"Build a better mousetrap and the world will beat a path to your door." The world may not beat a path to your door, but you'll have the pleasure at least of knowing that your bubble lasted longer. Here are some tricks to making better bubbles. They all start with the bubble solution.

Bubble Solutions

The most essential thing for making bubbles is a really good bubble solution. You could go to the corner toy store and buy a batch of bubble-making goop, but the homemade stuff is just as good, if not better. The other advantage of knowing how to make your own solution is that you can always have a batch around without spending your allowance on a commercial brand.

Depending on the kind of bubbles you want to make, you will need different solutions. Some recipes make really light bubbles, perfect for floating away on a lazy summer's day. Others make bubbles for sculpting; they are sturdier and won't float. Still others are a happy combination of the two.

Hints for Making Bubble Solution

Bubble solutions last for a long time if they are stored properly. You also want a clean solution, so try not to get too much dirt or gunk in the mixture. Sand particles will pop bubbles. If you can, make your solution a day or two ahead of time. You will get better, longer-lasting bubbles if you plan ahead. Using distilled water instead of tap water will give you a better bubble mixture. Some brands of dishwashing liquid work better than others. Often the most expensive brands work the best. Some bubble makers suggest using Dawn, Joy, or Ivory but other brands will work too; you may just need to add a bit more of the dish-washing liquid to the mixture. Glycerin can be purchased at most drugstores but corn syrup can be used as a substitute, if you prefer. All of these recipes can be made in larger or smaller amounts; just keep the same proportions of ingredients. If you leave the mixture out in the sun and the water evaporates, you may need to add a bit more water to replace it.

Warm Water or Cold Water

Try making your bubble solution with warm water and with cold water. See if the bubbles last longer if you change the temperature of the liquid solution.

Recipe 1
For everyday bubble-making fun

• • • • • •

1 cup dishwashing liquid

12 cups water

1 tablespoon glycerin

Mix the ingredients together. Remove any bubbles from the top of the liquid mixture.

Recipe 2
For bigger bubbles

• • • • • •

1 cup dishwashing liquid

8 cups water

1 tablespoon glycerin

Mix the ingredients together. Remove any bubbles from the top of the liquid mixture.

Recipe 3
For longer-lasting bubbles

• • • • • •

1 cup commercial bubble liquid (or try using recipes 1 or 2 above)

1 cup water

1 cup glycerin

Mix the ingredients together. Remove any bubbles from the top of the liquid mixture.

Techniques and Tools

You will need the following items to carry out the experiments in this book:

- baby shampoo
- baking soda
- cloth towels
- coat hangers
- cone-shaped paper drinking cups
- construction paper, black and white
- corn syrup
- gelatin
- glycerin
- hula hoop
- large tray (plastic or metal) or metal cookie sheet
- liquid dishwashing detergent such as Ivory, Palmolive, or Dawn
- milk cartons
- paper clips
- paper towels
- peppermint extract
- pipe cleaners
- plastic containers and bowls
- plastic fruit basket (the kind strawberries come in)
- plastic swimming pool/tub (optional)
- polystyrene (Styrofoam) drinking cups
- protractor
- ruler
- salt
- scissors
- stapler
- stopwatch or a watch with a second hand
- straws
- string
- sugar
- swimming or safety goggles
- tempera paints
- tin cans

The All-time Best Original All Natural Bubble Maker

Never go to the store again to buy a bubble blower. You have one close at hand. Hold out your arm and look at your hand. That's it. You've found your bubble blower!

a. How to blow bubbles with your fingers

You Will Need
- bubble solution
- a large, deep plastic bowl
- a towel
- water

What to Do

1. Take off all jewelry, as it may interfere with your bubble making.

2. Place your hand up to your wrist in the solution and make a fist.

3. Slowly remove your fist from the solution. Open your fist, leaving your thumb and fingers joined to form a circle. There should be a thin film of bubble solution in the space formed by this circle.

4. Hold your hand about 2 inches (5 cm) from your mouth and gently blow. A bubble should float from the other end of your hand.

5. Close your fingers into a fist, then open them again. Another soap film should appear. Keep blowing until the film stops forming. Re-dip your hand for more bubbles.

6. Instead of blowing a bubble, you can move your arm across your body and let the motion create the bubble.

7. Keep a towel and water handy, as hand-blown bubble solution tends to end up on your lips.

16

b. How to blow bubbles with your hands

This one is a little trickier. It may take some practice.

You Will Need

- bubble solution
- a large, deep plastic bowl
- a towel
- water
- a large plastic table

What to Do

METHOD 1

1. Dip both your hands up to your wrists in the bubble solution.

2. With your hands in the solution, touch the fingers of both hands together to form a large circle.

3. Remove your hands from the solution. There should be a soap film between your hands.

4. Hold your hands in front of your mouth and blow. Out comes a huge bubble.

5. Keep a towel and water handy, as the solution from hand-blown bubbles tends to end up on your lips.

METHOD 2

1. Cover the top of a flat plastic outdoor table with bubble solution.

2. Dip your hands up to your wrists in bubble solution, then place your hands on the surface of the table covered with solution.

3. Overlap your hands to create a small opening between your fingers. Blow into this opening, while slowly lifting your hands off the table. A bubble should form as you are doing this.

4. To finish off your bubble, join your hands together. The bubble should pop out from under your hands.

5. Keep a towel and water handy, as the solution from hand-blown bubbles tends to end up on your lips.

C. How to blow hand bubbles with two people

This trick will take a long time to perfect and will involve much laughter and a great quantity of bubble solution all over you, your friend, and your backyard.

You Will Need

- bubble solution
- a large, deep plastic bowl
- a towel
- water
- a large plastic table

What to Do

1. Dip both your hands up to your wrists in the bubble solution.

2. With your hands in the solution, touch your fingers together to form a large circle.

3. Remove your hands from the solution. There should be a soap film between your fingers.

4. Have your friend follow steps 1–3.

5. Stand facing your friend, leaving about 2 feet (60 cm) between you. At the same time, and at about the same height, start blowing a bubble, as you did in How to Blow Bubbles with Your Hands, Method 1, above.

How to Make a Bubble

You don't even have to blow to make a bubble. Dip your wand or bubble blower into solution and wave your arm in a sweeping motion. Bubbles will flow from your blower. For mouth blowing, say the word "plum" or "white" or "whoooosh" and you will get enough air to propel a bubble from a blower. Don't blow too hard or your bubble will burst. Be firm but gentle. Don't try to blow out a bubble as you would a birthday candle. That's too much force.

6. If all goes as planned, your friend's bubble will join up with yours to make one huge, tube-shaped bubble. Close off the bubble by bringing your hands together.

7. If it doesn't go well, you'll both have bubbles pop in your face.

A Bubble's Lifespan

Bubbles can last for a really long time. The record for the longest-lasting bubble could belong to you! Under ideal conditions bubbles have lasted for about a year. In 1917, Sir Thomas Dewar created a bubble that he kept for 108 days. A famous American bubble-blowing physics and chemistry teacher named Eiffel Plasterer (we kid you not!) blew a bubble that lasted 340 days.

Other Bubble Makers

You can use just about anything as a bubble blower. Look around your kitchen or bedroom. See anything made of plastic that has a hole in it? No? Try harder. How about an old CD that you don't use, or maybe a piece of costume jewelry or an empty plastic pen? All these things are perfect for creating bubbles.

Cups and cans

Push out the bottom of a polystyrene (Styrofoam) disposable cup. Dip one end of the cup into solution and blow a bubble out the other end. Or have an adult remove both ends of a tin can. Wrap both ends of the can with electrical tape to cover any sharp edges. Dip one end of the can into solution and blow a bubble. You can also wave the can to produce long, tube-like bubbles. This blower is also called a bubble tube (see Bubble Chains, page 44).

String and straw

Cut a 3-foot (1-meter) piece of string. Run the string through two straws, then tie the ends of the string together. Position the straws so that they form a "frame." Dip the string and the frame into a large container of bubble solution and blow through the resulting soap film.

Wands

Wire coat hangers make perfect bubble wands. Bend the coat hanger into a round, square, or funny shape and dip it into solution. Wave the wand to produce a bubble. Any kind of stiff wire can be used to make a wand.

Kitchen stuff

Grab an empty plastic fruit basket, the kind that strawberries come in, and dip it into solution. Wave or shake the basket to make bubbles. Or try the plastic form that holds a six-pack of soda.

Bubbles on a cookie sheet

Cookie sheets and plastic or metal trays are the best surfaces for experimenting with bubbles. They allow you to observe the bubbles closely without chasing them around and they confine the mess, making cleanup easier. Pour a layer of solution over the tray and blow bubbles onto it.

Trumpets or cones

Cut the ends off cone-shaped disposable cups. They make perfect bubble cones or trumpets. Dip the wide end of the trumpet into the solution and blow.

Quirky Bubbles

Bubble blowers can have all kinds of different shapes, even butterflies or flowers. No matter what shape your blower though, all the bubbles it forms will eventually be the same shape— a sphere. The bubble mixture forms an elastic film around the air you blow. Nature is extremely economical, so the soap film always takes the smallest shape—that with the smallest possible surface area. And the shape that holds the greatest volume of air within the smallest surface area is a sphere.

Big Bubble Makers

These are a bit of a challenge to make and you may have to scout for materials.

You Will Need

- PVC tubing (available at plumbing supply or hardware stores), about 3 feet long by 1 inch in diameter (1 m x 2.5 cm) (have them cut it for you)
- 2 caps to fit the ends of the PVC tubing
- 2 small, round metal binder rings, the kind found in stationery stores
- 6–8 feet (2 to 2.5 m) of cotton upholstery/drapery fabric trim, about 1 inch (2.5 cm) wide
- an adult helper
- a large, deep bucket
- bubble solution

What to Do

1. Tie together the ends of the fabric trim and place the knot inside one end of the tube. Use one cap to close off the end of the tube, holding the fabric flat inside the tubing.

2. Place one metal binder ring through the loop of fabric you have just created; then close the ring around the tube. Place the other metal ring around the fabric loop and allow it to slide freely; this ring will serve as a weight to maintain control of your bubble maker.

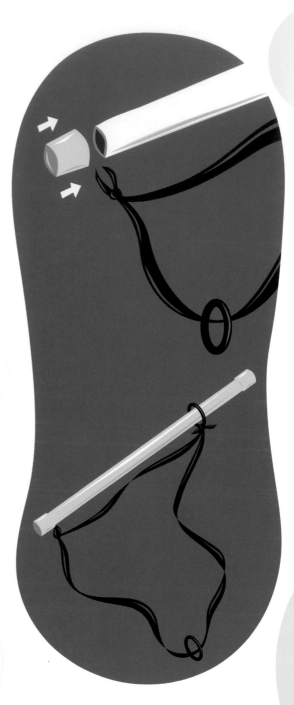

3. Cap off the other end of the tubing.

4. Gather the material at the fabric-capped end and dunk the material and the end of the wand into a bucket filled with bubble solution.

5. Remove the wand from the bucket, allowing the excess to drip back into the bucket, and gently pull back the ring on the tube to expose a film of solution on the fabric. Hold the wand away from you and allow a gust of air to push against the film.

6. As soon as you see a bulge of bubble on the wand, move the ring back toward the fabric-capped end. This will make a giant, floating bubble.

7. If you want to make a tube bubble, begin to walk slowly and watch a huge long bubble form behind you.

8. Stand on the crest of a hill. The wind may push a huge long bubble from your wand.

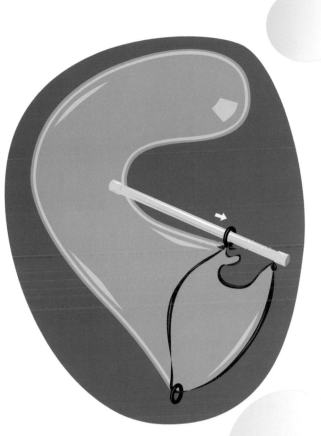

The Longest Bubble

A bubble over 100 feet long has been documented; it was created using a commercial bubble blower.

Bubble Trouble Shooting

Some days you just can't make a bubble no matter how hard you try. Never fear—here's a bubble trouble guide.

Problem

I can't get a bubble to form on my bubble blower.

Solution

Your solution may be too weak. Add a small amount of glycerin and liquid detergent to the solution. Gently stir and let sit for several minutes.

You may not have put enough solution on the blower. Re-dip your bubble blower in the solution and leave it there a moment before blowing.

If you're blowing bubbles outdoors, the solution may be evaporating in the sun. Move to the shade.

Problem

I can't make a big bubble. I only get tiny bubbles.

Solution

Try holding the blower farther away from your lips. Blow lightly.

Look at your bubble solution. Is the surface covered with tiny bubbles? Dip your blower into an area free of bubbles. Try not to stir up your solution, as it will make the surface foamy.

Problem

My bubbles pop as soon as I start to blow them.

Solution

Your bubbles may be hitting a dry surface. Make sure all the surfaces are wet.

Your solution may be too weak.

If it's too windy outside, dirt may be popping the bubbles. Move to a more sheltered area.

Check your solution. Does it have dirt, grass, or pebbles in it? Run your solution through a sieve to get rid of the gunk.

Problem

My bubble sticks to the blower. I want the bubble to float in the air.

Solution

Here's a technique that bubble aficionados (people who love bubbles) use to detach a bubble from a blower: twist your wrist so the bubble floats off the end of the blower. Be patient. It will take some practice.

Bubble Skin ⊘

*t*ake a look at a bubble. Not much to it…or is there? Take a look again.

You Will Need

- a bubble wand
- a tray or cookie sheet
- bubble solution
- a straw

What to Do

1. Dip your wand into the bubble solution. Take a close look at the surface of the film on the wand. What do you see? Now gently blow on the surface. What happens?

2. Dip your wand into the bubble solution again. This time instead of blowing a bubble into the air, blow a bubble onto the surface of a dry cookie sheet. What happens to the bubble?

3. Cover the cookie sheet with a thin layer of bubble solution. Make sure the entire surface is wet. Now try blowing another bubble onto the surface of the cookie sheet. What happens to the bubble this time?

4. Dip a straw into the bubble solution and blow a bubble onto the cookie sheet. What shape is the bubble?

5. Dip your wand into the bubble solution and blow a bubble into the air. Catch the bubble with your hand. Does it pop? Try it again after wetting your hand with the bubble solution. Does this make a difference?

What Happened

When you dipped the wand into the solution, a thin soap film formed on it. This film, or membrane, is actually a thin layer of water between two layers of air. If you looked closely, you could see different colors swirl on the surface of the film. When you blew onto the surface, the film gathered together to form a spherical bubble, which floated away from the wand.

The bubble film will always try to enclose the greatest volume (amount of space or air) inside the smallest surface area possible—and a sphere is the shape that does that. Even if your bubble starts out a different shape it will eventually end up being a sphere, unless it pops first.

In the second step, you discovered that bubbles burst when they hit a dry surface. This is because the fragile soap-and-water "skin" of the bubble dries when it hits the surface and breaks. It's similar to a pin bursting a balloon—all the air escapes through the hole. When the bubble touched a wet surface (step 3), the bubble didn't burst; instead, it attached itself to the surface of the cookie sheet.

In step 4 you learned an exception to the rule: bubbles don't always form spheres. They may form half spheres, or hemispheres, when they come in contact with a flat wet surface.

27

The Life of a Bubble

Your bubble begins its life as part of a slippery solution. As soon as you gather the soap film on a bubble blower, it's simply a matter of time until the bubble pops. But how much time?

You Will Need

- bubble solution
- bubble blowers
- a tray or cookie sheet
- a plastic outdoor table
- several sheets of black construction paper
- several sheets of white construction paper
- a sheet of white paper or cardboard
- masking tape
- a watch with a second hand
- a helper

What to Do

1. Tape the sheets of black construction paper together to form a ring. This will protect your bubble. Make a second ring using the white paper.

2. Cover the tray or sheet with a thin layer of bubble solution. Make sure the entire surface is wet.

3. Dip your straw into the solution and blow a small bubble onto the tray.

4. Place the black paper ring around the bubble. Have a helper hold the white cardboard slightly above the bubble, leaving enough space for you to observe the swirls of color on the top of the bubble.

5. Watch the top of the bubble closely and make note of the color changes you see. What color is the top of the bubble before it pops? Do this several times. Does the bubble always have the same sequence of colors before it pops? Use the second hand on a watch to time how long it takes for the bubble to pop.

6. Try this activity using the white paper ring. Does this make it easier or harder to see the colors on the bubbles?

7. Change the bubble solution you're using. Does more liquid soap make the bubbles last longer? How about more glycerin?

What Happened

The surface swirled with different colors. The colors you observed were green, blue, magenta, and yellow. The color changes may have occurred several times, always in that order, before the colors seemed to disappear and you saw only a milky white, with what looked like spots dappling the bubble's surface. Then the bubble was gone. The colors of the bubble tell you something about the thickness of its skin. When light hits a soap bubble, most of the light goes right through it, but some of the light gets reflected, or bounced back, from both the outside and inside surfaces of the bubble skin. The reflections get mixed together in a process called "thin film interference," which causes the light to change and give off different colors. These are the colors you see when you look at the bubble. The colors will change with the thickness of the soap film, which gets progressively thinner as it ages. When the film gets really thin, the top of the bubble will appear black in front of a black background.

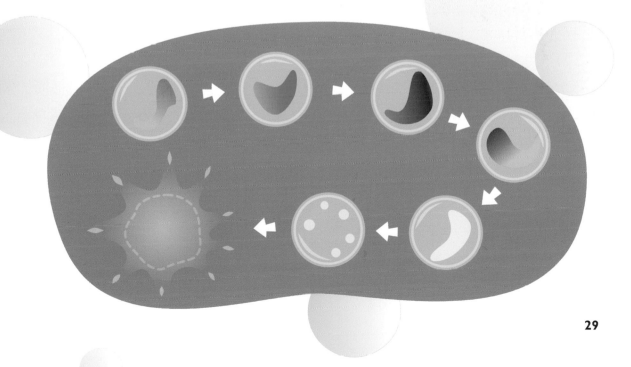

Bubble-Eating Bubbles

*d*o bubbles ever get hungry? Would they "eat" or swallow another bubble for dinner? See if you can explain where the tiny bubble disappears to when it meets a bigger bubble.

You Will Need

- bubble solution
- a straw
- a tray or cookie sheet

What to Do

1. Coat the entire surface of the tray or sheet carefully with a thin layer of bubble solution.

2. Dip your straw into the solution and blow a small bubble onto the tray.

3. Dip your straw into the solution again and blow a large bubble next to the small bubble. Watch what happens when the two bubbles meet.

4. Try this again, this time blowing two medium bubbles about the same size. What do the bubbles do now?

5. Now try blowing two small bubbles. Is there any difference in the way they behave compared to the large, same-sized bubbles?

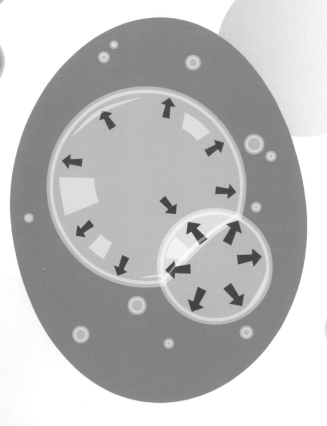

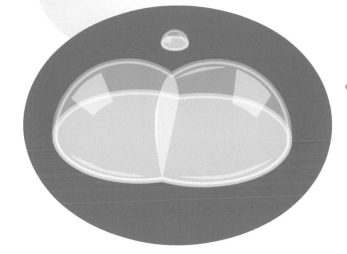

What Happened

When the big bubble came in contact with the little bubble, the little bubble pushed into the larger bubble. When two bubbles of similar size were next to each other, they came together and were separated by a thin "wall." The bubbles hold their shape because the air inside them is under greater pressure than the air outside, and it pushes the soap film outward. The smaller the bubble, the greater the air pressure inside. Thus, when a smaller bubble touches against a bigger bubble, the greater air pressure forces the smaller bubble to push into the bigger bubble. When two bubbles of the same size touch each other on the tray, they push against each other with equal force and the film forms a straight "wall" between them. Sometimes, if two bubbles sit next to each other long enough, they will join together into one bigger bubble.

Bubble Bees

When you look at a mass of bubbles, does it have a slightly familiar pattern? Have you seen this shape somewhere before? Let's see if this will jog your memory.

You Will Need

- a tray or cookie sheet
- a clear, thin sheet of rigid plastic (the top of an old CD case is perfect)
- 24 pennies
- a straw
- bubble solution

What to Do

1. Coat the entire surface of the tray or sheet carefully with a thin layer of bubble solution.

2. Place four stacks of six pennies in a square on the tray.

3. Wet one side of the plastic sheet and place the sheet on the stacks of pennies.

4. Use a straw to blow tiny bubbles under the sheet of plastic. What happens to the bubbles? How many sides do the bubbles have?

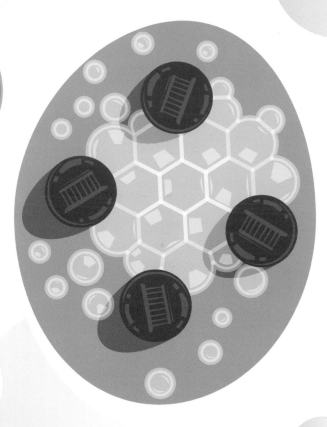

32

What Happened

The more you blew, the more bubbles you created. Soon the bubbles joined together to form something that looked like the honeycomb in beehives. The bubbles were no longer spherical; instead, they had six sides. When a bunch of bubbles are squished together, each bubble tries to form a sphere, but the spheres push against each other. When bubbles meet on a flat surface, only three bubbles will touch at any one point; they push all other bubbles aside. If all of your bubbles are around the same size, you end up with the six-sided, or hexagonal, shape. Again, this shape allows the most air inside the smallest surface area. Bees know this too; that is why they make honeycomb in this distinctive shape.

Bubble Angles

As you have seen in Bubble Bees and Bubble-Eating Bubbles, bubbles don't mind changing their shape. Can you predict at what angle one bubble will join another, regardless of its size?

You Will Need

- bubble solution
- a straw
- a tray or cookie sheet
- a plastic protractor

What to Do

1. Coat the entire surface of the tray or sheet carefully with a thin layer of bubble solution.

2. Dip your straw into the solution and blow three medium-sized bubbles, so they join each other in the center.

3. Dip a protractor into the bubble solution so that it is completely covered. Slide the protractor under the bubbles and measure the angle at which the bubbles meet.

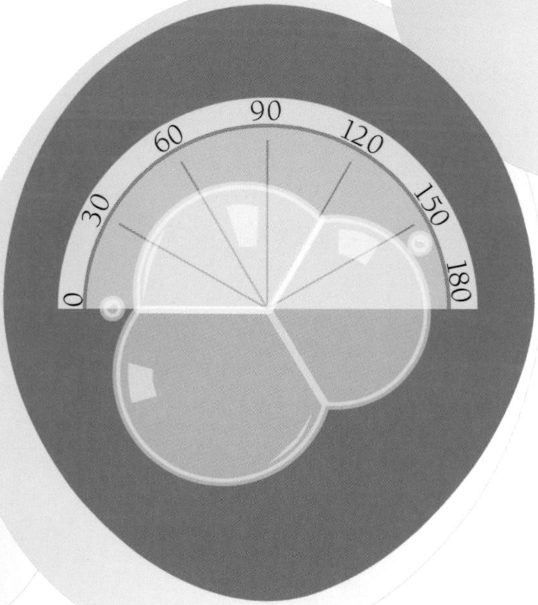

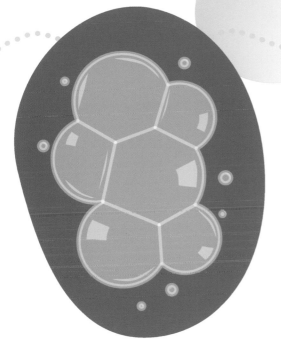

What Happened

No matter how large or small the bubbles were, when they joined together they produced the same angle, 120 degrees. As you saw in Bubble Bees (page 32), when bubbles join together they meet so that the walls of three bubbles come into contact with each other. A fourth bubble will always get pushed to one side. If you divide a circle into three equal wedges, each wedge has a 120-degree angle. This is the angle the bubbles will form with each other, even if the bubbles are of different sizes.

4. Blow an entire plateful of bubbles, so that many bubbles are joined together as in Bubble Bees. Measure the angles where the bubbles join each other. Is the angle the same as the one where the three bubbles joined in step 3?

Bubbles in a Glass

*C*all it a hunch, but we bet that at some point in your short life an adult has probably told you not to blow bubbles in your milk. Here's a way to do it without getting into too much trouble.

You Will Need

- 2 straws
- 2 clear glasses
- bubble solution
- plain, chocolate, or other milk, such as soy or lactose-free
- a stopwatch or a watch with a second hand

What to Do

1. Fill a glass halfway with bubble solution.

2. Place the straw in the glass and blow into it to create bubbles. Take a close look at the bubbles. How are they joined together?

3. Fill another glass halfway with milk and blow into it with a straw. Do these bubbles look the same as the soap bubbles?

4. Use a stopwatch or a watch with a second hand to find the time it takes for the bubbles in each glass to burst. Which last longer, the bubbles in soap or in milk?

What Happened

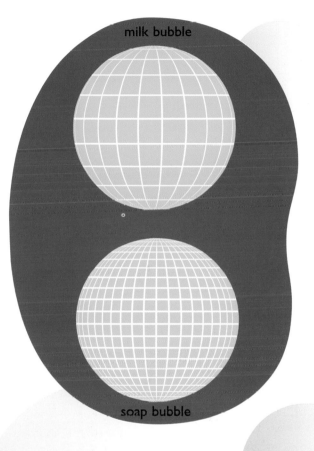

milk bubble

soap bubble

The soap bubbles lasted longer than the milk bubbles. When you blew into the straw, bubbles formed in the  liquid. Both soap and milk are made up of small particles called molecules; these molecules assemble themselves into a film to enclose the air you blew into the milk and soap. The molecules in milk don't create as stable a bond as the molecules in the soap, so the milk bubbles burst more easily.

Bubbles for All Seasons

While it's true that you can blow bubbles at any time of year, both indoors and out, there are certain weather conditions that bubbles prefer.

If you're blowing bubbles on a warm day, try to stick to the shade. Bright sun makes your bubbles dry out and pop faster. Hot, humid days are better for longer-lasting bubbles than scorching, dry days. And if you're really adventuresome, try blowing bubbles on a cold winter day. Your hands may freeze, but the bubbles will last a long time.

Cloudy days are great for blowing bubbles. And bubbles last even longer right after it rains. Early morning and dusk are perfect times for creating the biggest bubbles. In case you don't believe that bubbles really react to the weather, we'll prove our point.

You Will Need
- bubble solution
- a sunny window or lamp
- a clear plastic container
- plastic wrap
- a straw
- a bowl
- a shower
- a watch with a second hand
- an adult helper

What to Do

1. Fill a small transparent plastic container with bubble solution to coat its interior, then pour out most of the solution. Leave a thin layer of solution on the bottom and make sure the solution wets the lip of the container.

2. Place a straw in the container and blow bubbles. Wet the plastic wrap with bubble solution and place it over the top of the container.

3. Put the container in the freezer section of your fridge and, leaving the freezer door open, time how long it takes for the bubbles to pop.

4. Repeat steps 1 and 2, then place the container in bright sunlight or under a lamp. How long do your bubbles last this time?

5. Ask an adult to run a hot shower to make the bathroom steamy. Leave the container in the room. How long do the bubbles last under these conditions?

What Happened

The bubbles resting in the sun burst the most quickly. The warmth and dryness there evaporated the water in the solution. The cooler air in the freezer kept the bubble mixture from drying out as fast, so the bubbles took longer to pop. Steamy conditions are the best for longer-lasting bubbles. The water in the air—the steam— keeps the bubble mixture from drying out so the bubbles last longer.

Bubble Tricks

Can you believe there are some really neat tricks you can do with bubbles? Okay, a bubble can't "fetch" like your dog, but it can do things your pet can't. See what we mean as you try the next three experiments.

Bubble Inside a Bubble

*L*et's see if you can blow one bubble inside another.

You Will Need

- bubble solution
- a straw
- a tray or cookie sheet

What to Do

1. Cover the bottom of a tray or cookie sheet with a thin layer of bubble solution. Make sure the solution coats the entire surface.

2. Dip the bottom 2 inches (5 cm) of the straw into the solution to wet it.

3. Blow a bubble through the straw onto the tray. When you have a medium-sized bubble (about 3 inches [7.5 cm] in diameter), gently withdraw the straw from the bubble.

4. Coat the end of your straw in bubble solution again. Make sure the straw is really wet.

5. Gently poke the straw through the first bubble and blow a second bubble inside the first, onto the tray. Blow only a small bubble.

What Happened

You created a bubble inside a bubble.

40

Person Inside a Bubble

If you have ever wondered what it's like inside a bubble, here's your chance to find out!

You Will Need

- a hula hoop
- a plastic outdoor swimming tub
- lots of bubble solution
- swimming or safety goggles
- several adult helpers

What to Do

This activity is obviously best for a hot summer day. And it's a good idea to wear a bathing suit.

1. Fill the tub with bubble solution about 3 inches (7.5 cm) deep.

2. Lay the hula hoop in the swimming tub to cover it with solution.

3. Step carefully into the swimming tub and stand in the center of the hula hoop. We recommend goggles in case of bubble bursts.

4. Have your helpers wet their hands thoroughly in bubble solution up to the wrist.

5. Standing on opposite sides of the hula hoop, have the helpers slowly pick it up and lift it straight over your head.

Note: If every part of you is soaking wet—your body, your hair, your swimsuit—you could try walking through the bubble. Chances are it will pop, but it'll be fun trying. Remember, don't jump into a swimming pool if you're covered with bubble solution!

What Happened

Now you know what it's like to be inside a bubble.

Bubbles with Holes

Generally when you poke your finger through a bubble film, it pops. But here's a trick that will surprise even the most experienced bubble fanatic.

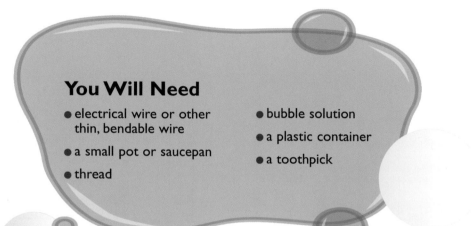

You Will Need

- electrical wire or other thin, bendable wire
- a small pot or saucepan
- thread
- bubble solution
- a plastic container
- a toothpick

What to Do

1. Use a piece of wire longer than the circumference of the pot; the excess will be the handle. Wrap the wire around the sides of the pot to create a perfect circle and twist the ends together.

2. Cut a piece of thread about 6 inches (15 cm) long and tie a knot at one end of it to form a big loop.

Leave enough thread so that you can tie it onto the wire bubble wand at the other end.

3. Dip the bubble blower into a deep container of bubble solution. Raise it upright with the thread loop hanging inside the wire circle. Your blower should have a thin film of bubble solution covering it; the thread loop should be hanging on this film.

4. Poke a toothpick or your finger into the middle of the thread loop. What happens?

What Happened

A hole appeared in the middle of the loop—a perfect circle surrounded by a soap film around the edge of the thread loop. When you dipped the wire circle into the solution, it formed a disk of film across the circle. The soap film is elastic and it tries to maintain the smallest possible surface area. When an opening is made inside the thread loop, the film no longer needs to cover that space. The film shrinks back, pulling the thread loop into a circle, again giving the new region of film the smallest possible surface area.

Bubble Chains

You can't lock up your bike with this chain, but you'll have fun making it.

You Will Need

- bubble solution
- a straw or tin can bubble blower (also called a bubble tube, see page 20)
- a helper

What to Do

1. Dip the end of your straw or bubble tube into the solution. Blow a bubble and flick it off the end of the tube.

2. Catch the bubble back on the end of the blower.

3. Have a friend dip a straw into the bubble solution and blow a bubble on the bottom of the first bubble.

4. Hold the bubble blower
steady as your friend
begins to add bubbles
to the chain by repeat-
ing step 3. How many
bubbles can you add
before the chain breaks?

5. Trade places; while your
friend holds the tube, you
make the chain.

What Happened

You created a bubble chain.

Measuring Bubbles

*"**M**y bubble is bigger than yours."*

"Is not!"

"Is too!"

"Is not!"

Stop! There's a simple way to prove who has the bigger bubble.

You Will Need

- a plastic ruler or measuring stick
- bubble solution
- your favorite bubble blower
- a plastic outdoor table
- a measuring tape

What to Do

1. Completely cover the surface of a plastic table with bubble solution. Remember, when a bubble hits a dry surface, it will burst.

2. Blow your best bubble onto the table's surface using your favorite bubble blower.

3. Wet the ruler or measuring stick with bubble solution and slide the ruler through the bubble. Measure both the width and height of the bubble with the ruler.

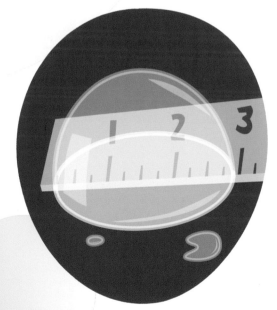

4. Be sure the table surface is wet with bubble solution. Blow another bubble onto the tabletop and, this time, pop the bubble. The bubble will leave a "ring," which you can also measure for diameter (the width of the bubble).

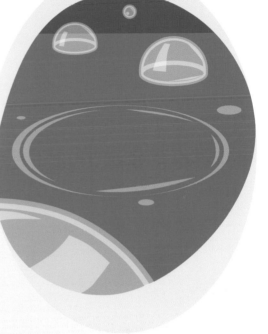

What Happened

You were able to blow a huge bubble and have proof of its size. The wet ruler slid through the bubble to give you an accurate measurement of it. Were domed bubbles the same width as their height?

Giant Bubbles

*t*o be politically correct, you might want to call these "soap-film-enhanced" or "girth-challenged" bubbles. Whatever you call them, these bubbles are enormous!

You Will Need

- a plastic outdoor swimming tub
- a hula hoop
- about 10 feet (3 m) of cotton drapery edging
- 4 pieces of wood lathing, about 1 inch (2.5 cm) wide by 3 feet (1 m) long
- a stapler
- 3 friends
- an adult helper
- a plastic outdoor table
- straws

What to Do

Method 1

1. Add enough bubble solution to fill the swimming tub about 3 inches (7.5 cm) deep.

2. Lay the hula hoop in the tub so that it is covered with bubble solution.

3. Wet your hands up to the wrist with bubble solution and have a friend do the same.

4. Stand on opposite sides of the hula hoop. On the count of 3, take the hula hoop from the bubble solution and raise it to vertical. It should be covered with a layer of soap film.

5. Start walking side by side, holding the hoop between you. The soap film should start forming a huge bubble behind you.

This one takes extreme coordination and cooperation among the four participants.

1. Tie the ends of the cotton drapery edging together to form a circle.

2. Have an adult staple or tie big knots into the edging at 2.5-foot (75-cm) intervals to create 4 evenly spaced "handles."

3. Dip the fabric "wand" into the swimming tub.

4. Each participant takes a handle and together, on the count of three, they lift the wand from the tub. Hold the handles apart to spread out the fabric wand to its full size, producing an enormous soap-bubble film.

5. Wait for a gust of wind or take several steps to create an airflow that will blow the bubble.

1. Cover the surface of a large plastic outdoor table with bubble solution.

2. Dip a straw into bubble solution and blow a large bubble on the surface of the table.

3. While you are blowing your bubble, have your friends dip straws into bubble solution, put the ends of their straws into your bubble, and blow to make your bubble bigger. How big can the bubble get before it pops?

4. Have a friend start a new bubble while you and your other friends help blow with your dipped straws.

What Happened

Whatever method you used, you should have been able to make some mighty healthy bubbles.

Printing with Bubbles

You can create beautiful works of art with bubbles. Frame these pictures and ask people to guess how you painted such interesting patterns.

You Will Need

- bubble solution
- a metal tray or cookie sheet
- straws or bubble blowers
- tempera paint
- food coloring
- paper

What to Do

1. Pour some bubble solution onto the tray, making sure to cover the entire surface.
2. Add a few drops of food coloring or tempera paints to different areas of the tray.
3. Use a straw to create mounds of bubbles. Try to make the bubbles a variety of sizes.
4. Place a piece of paper over the bubbles; this will pop them and leave behind a print.

What Happened

The dry paper popped the bubbles,
making a color print.

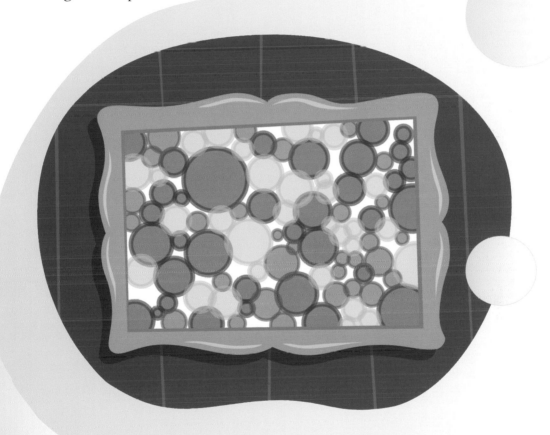

Centipede Bubble Chains

here's a silly creation that you can make by yourself or with several of your friends.

You Will Need

- bubble solution
- several straws
- a plastic outdoor table or large cookie sheet
- several friends

What to Do

1. Cover the surface of the table with a thin layer of bubble solution.

2. Dip your straw into the bubble solution and blow a bubble on the surface of the table.

3. Blow a second bubble some distance away about the same size as the first.

4. Have your friends blow more bubbles to fill the space between the two with new bubbles until you have created a "centipede." How long does your bubble centipede last?

What Happened

The bubbles joined together into a shape. You can make all kinds of funny shapes, like hearts, initials, or silly faces!

Bubble Bounce

*Y*ou can't play basketball with these bubble balls—
you'd be caught "dribbling." See how long you can keep
a bubble in the air.

You Will Need

- bubble solution
- a small and a medium-sized bubble wand
- a piece of cardboard or a small folded paper fan

What to Do

1. Dip your wand into the bubble solution and blow a bubble. Flick the bubble off the wand to float it in the air.

2. Wave the fan or cardboard from side to side under the floating bubble to keep it from falling to the ground.

3. Dip your wand again and, this time, blow several bubbles into the air. Try to fan or wave the second or third bubble to come off the wand. Is it easier to keep this bubble aloft?

4. Try different solutions. Do some solutions make bubbles that are easier to keep afloat?

What Happened

The first bubble blown from the bubble blower was the most difficult to keep afloat. This is because it contained the most solution and so was heavier. Each successive bubble (from a single dip) is lighter than the one before and is easier to keep floating.

Bubble Ghosts

*b*ubble, bubble, toil and trouble.… *Try this fun and spooky experiment. Ghostly gases use mysterious powers to hold your bubbles in place.*

You Will Need

- bubble solution
- bubble blowers or wands
- a deep kitchen sink
- baking soda
- white vinegar
- a deep pie plate or plastic container
- a chair to stand on if you are too short to see into the kitchen sink (optional)
- an adult helper

What to Do

1. Place the stopper in the kitchen sink. Have an adult help you place the pie plate in the sink and put about ½ cup (125 mL) of baking soda into it.

2. Pour about 1 cup (250 mL) of vinegar onto the baking soda. You should now have your basic volcano in a sink.

3. When the "volcano" has stopped erupting, begin to blow bubbles over the top of the sink. Don't blow the bubbles into the sink!

4. Watch what happens as the bubbles begin to drop into the sink.

5. When you are finished, simply rinse out the sink and the container with water.

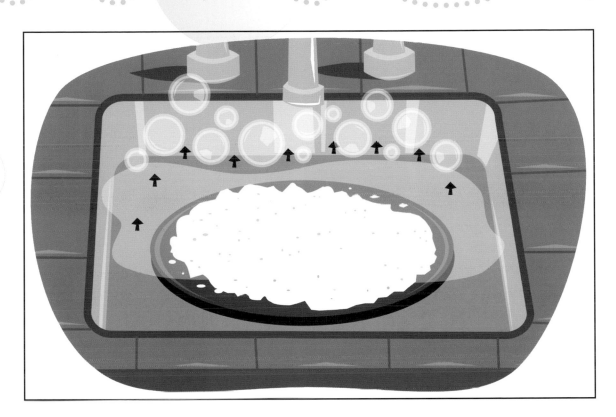

What Happened

When you combined the baking soda with the vinegar, you produced a colorless, odorless gas called carbon dioxide.

This gas is heavier than air, so it stayed at the bottom of the sink. Bubbles that would normally fall were held in place by the carbon dioxide gas.

Whales and Bubbles

Did you know that bubbles could be used to "hunt"? According to the experts at the Vancouver Public Aquarium, humpback whales in Alaska use a technique called "bubble net feeding" to gather krill, minute shrimplike creatures that are the mainstay of their diet. Several humpbacks coordinate to swim in a circle while blowing bubbles; this creates a wall through which the tiny krill cannot escape. Then the whales simply swim up through the middle of the ring, gulping their dinner.

Bad News About Bubbles

SCUBA stands for Self Contained Underwater Breathing Apparatus. Scuba divers use metal tanks containing compressed air to allow them to breathe under water. Water is more dense than air and, the greater its depth, the greater the water's density. The molecules in deep water are closer together and the collective force they exert produces greater pressure. At great depths, the pressure can be extreme. When divers go deep under oceans and lakes, they have to think carefully about bubbles. The direction in which their bubbles travel tells them which way is up. They must blow bubbles as they ascend because the air in their lungs is under greater pressure when they are deeper in the water. If they don't blow out this air in time, their lungs may burst! Another condition called "the bends," or decompression sickness, is caused by bubbles of nitrogen gas that form in the blood if a diver comes up too quickly. To prevent this, divers must be careful about how deep they dive and how long

they spend at each depth. Large boxes called recompression chambers are used to cure the bends. The diver sits in the chamber where greater air pressure allows the nitrogen to be absorbed back into the blood. Then the pressure is gradually reduced until the diver is back at normal air pressure.

Bubble Bath

Your first experience with bubbles probably came in the form of a bubble bath. It was a great trick your parents did to get you to jump into the tub. Now you can make your own bubble bath solution and keep it in a special container. Maybe you can even get your parents to take a dip with your custom-made bubble bath.

You Will Need

- a plastic bowl
- a measuring cup
- a spoon
- a plastic bottle with a cap
- ½ cup (125 mL) bottled water
- 2½ tablespoons (38mL) of shampoo
- 1 tablespoon (15mL) of glycerin
- ¼ teaspoon (1mL) salt (use table salt, not rock or kosher salt)
- a drop of perfume or 1 tablespoon (15mL) of rose water (available in specialty food stores)
- a drop of food coloring
- a funnel
- an adult helper

What to Do

1. Ask an adult before using any perfumes. Pour all the above ingredients into the bowl and stir to combine.

2. Place the funnel into the top of the plastic bottle and, with an adult's help, pour the liquid into the bottle. Put the cap on the bottle and store in a safe place.

3. Use only a tablespoon of the liquid for your bath.

Note: If you have sensitive skin, place a small amount of the bubble bath on your wrist. If you break out in a rash, don't use the bubble bath.

Bubbles on the Level

Your eyes can play tricks on you. Sometimes you may think something is "level," or flat, when it's really on an angle. How can you tell if something is really flat? Use a bubble!

You Will Need

- a carpenter's level

What to Do

1. Place a carpenter's level on various surfaces around your house. Ask an adult to help you see whether the item (a picture, the floor, a countertop) is level.

2. Hold the level at different angles and see what happens to the bubble inside the vial. What does the bubble do when the level is on a flat surface?

What Happened

A carpenter's level is a pretty handy little tool for everyone from construction crews who build houses to people who simply want to hang pictures. As you saw, the bubble in the level showed whether a surface was straight or not. The vial in the level contains a special liquid that nearly fills the tube, leaving only a small bubble at the top. When the level is placed in different positions, the bubble moves within the vial. When the bubble is between the two lines, it means the surface is even. If one end or the other is up even a little bit, the bubble will move up on that side. This shows very quickly which side is higher.

Science Museum Bubbles

Sometimes in science museums or classroom demonstrations, special plastic shapes are used as bubble blowers. Aside from creating some of the most interesting bubble shapes you've ever seen, they demonstrate the science of bubbles very well. The strangest thing is the way the bubbles behave after the bubble blower is covered with solution.

You Will Need

- pipe cleaners
- a large, deep bowl for dipping blowers
- bubble solution
- sharp scissors
- an adult helper

What to Do

1. Have an adult help you cut pipe cleaners into 3-inch (7.5-cm) pieces. Make bubble blowers in the following shapes:

   ✓ cube

   ✓ tetrahedron

   ✓ 2 intersecting circles

   ✓ pyramid

2. Immerse the bubble shape completely in the bubble solution.

3. Slowly pull the bubble shape from the liquid and hold it steady. Do not wave the bubble maker in the air.

4. Carefully watch the soap film on the bubble shape to see what happens.

What Happened

The film on the bubble maker did the strangest thing: it stretched and pulled itself to create new bubbles inside the bubble maker. As always, the soap film took the shape with the smallest surface area.

Bubbles and Your Breath

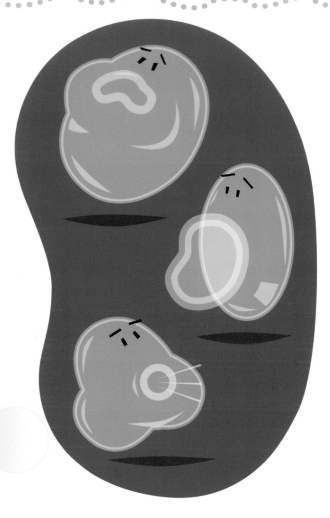

What do you think will blow a better bubble—your breath or a turkey baster? That's a pretty silly question now, isn't it? The answer may surprise you.

You Will Need
- bubble solution
- a straw
- a turkey baster
- a tray or cookie sheet
- a watch with a second hand

What to Do

1. Wet the cookie sheet thoroughly with a thin layer of bubble solution.

2. Dip your straw into the solution and blow a medium-sized bubble on the sheet. Use your watch to time how long the bubble lasts.

3. Dip the end of the turkey baster into the solution and blow another bubble about the same size as the one you blew with the straw. Time how long this bubble lasts.

What Happened

The bubble you blew with the turkey baster lasted longer. The difference between the two bubbles is the gases in them. They both contain oxygen, nitrogen, and carbon dioxide, but in different proportions. Carbon dioxide dissolves very easily in water—in fact, more easily than it does in air—but nitrogen and oxygen do not. There is a much greater proportion of carbon dioxide in your breath than in the air around you (and in the turkey baster), so the bubble you blew by mouth has more carbon dioxide than the turkey baster bubble. The greater proportion of carbon dioxide in the mouth-blown bubble dissolves more quickly in the bubble skin, which is chiefly water. This makes the skin less "sticky," so its molecules hold together less well and it bursts more quickly.

Edible Bubbles

While bubble solution tastes yucky, there are some bubbles that taste a little better. When we say edible, we don't mean you can make a meal of the solution or drink it through a straw, but you can safely pop these bubbles with your tongue.

You Will Need

- 2 teaspoons (10 mL) concentrated baby shampoo
- 1 tablespoon (15 mL) corn syrup
- 1 cup (250 mL) water
- a drop of peppermint extract (optional)
- a small container
- a spoon
- a bubble blower

What to Do

1. Place the baby shampoo, corn syrup, and water in a container and use a spoon to mix the ingredients together.

2. Dip your favorite bubble blower into the concoction and blow a bubble.

3. Chase the bubble as it floats around the room and use your tongue to pop it. How does it taste?

4. Try adding a drop of peppermint extract to the solution and pop another bubble.

5. Don't eat too many bubbles as you might get a tummy ache.

What Happened

The corn syrup turned a yucky taste into a slightly yummy one. The syrup acted like the glycerin in the basic solution to make the bubbles stronger. Sometimes after you add the peppermint extract, it's hard to get bubbles to form; this is because the extract contains oils or alcohol that stop the soap from forming a film. If you found it hard to make bubbles, try adding a little bit more shampoo.

Bubble Candy

there is a wonderful candy filled with bubbles that feels like an edible sponge on your tongue. When this amber-colored treat is covered with chocolate, it becomes an old-fashioned confection sometimes called seafoam or honeycomb. Grab an apron and an adult helper and make some bubbly candy.

You Will Need

- a heavy 4-quart (3.785-l) saucepan with tall sides
- 3 cups (750 mL) sugar
- 1½ cups (325 mL) golden corn syrup
- ¼ tsp (1 mL) salt
- 1 tsp (5 mL) unflavored gelatin
- 1 tbsp (15 mL) cold water
- a small bowl
- 1 tbsp (15 mL) baking soda
- a wooden spoon
- a candy thermometer
- 10-inch (25-cm) square pan
- butter or margarine
- an adult helper

What to Do

Note: The candy mixture is very hot and can cause serious burns. Make certain an adult uses caution when preparing the mixture. Do not touch the candy until it is cool.

1. Pour the sugar, syrup, and salt into the saucepan and stir to mix.

2. Have an adult place the saucepan on the stove and cook over medium heat. Stir the mixture until the sugar dissolves.

3. While the adult is busy stirring the mixture, place the gelatin in a small bowl and add the water. Stir to mix.

4. Prepare the pan by using a small amount of butter or margarine to grease the bottom.

5. When the mixture in the saucepan is clear, have an adult increase the heat to medium-high. Have an adult use a candy thermometer to measure the temperature of the boiling syrup. Be careful toward the end of cooking (270–280 degrees); have the adult stir the mixture occasionally.

6. When the candy reaches 290 degrees F (145 degrees C), have an adult remove it from the heat very quickly to prevent scorching.

7. Off the heat, have the adult add the baking soda, stir gently (so as not to stop the foaming action), then add the gelatin. Have the adult continue to stir the candy gently for several minutes, then pour the mixture into the greased pan. Do not spread the foamy mixture; allow it to cool undisturbed for at least 1 hour.

8. Crush into small pieces (by placing a sheet of wax paper over the top and tapping or rolling with a rolling pin). If you wish, you can melt chocolate and drip it over the candy. Store the candy in an airtight container.

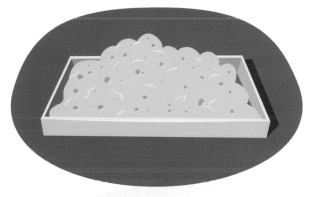

What Happened

As soon as the baking soda was added, the mixture started bubbling. The bubbles formed because the baking soda, a chemical called sodium bicarbonate, gives off carbon dioxide gas when it is heated. This gas becomes trapped in the heated mixture and forms millions of tiny bubbles. When the candy hardens, the bubbles make it really crunchy.

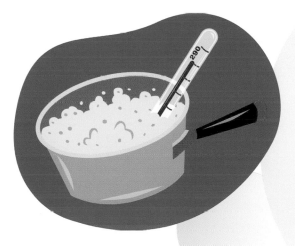

71

Bubbles in Food

Bubbles can be found in all sorts of food. Take for example the holes in Swiss cheese. No, it isn't a tiny mouse eating round sections out of the cheese. Cheese contains bacteria that give off carbon dioxide gas; as the cheese ripens, the gas forms bubbles. The cheese hardens around these bubbles, and that pretty much accounts for the holes. And now for some really interesting Swiss cheese trivia: the US government has regulations strictly controlling the size of the holes, or "eyes," for Grade A Swiss cheese. If the holes are too big or too small, it can't be called Grade A.

Bubbles in Soda

The next time you drink a carbonated beverage, take a close look at the liquid. You should see tiny bubbles rising from the bottom of the glass or bottle. Take a sniff over the top of the glass. Does your nose tickle? The bubbles rising from your drink contain a gas called carbon dioxide. It's these bubbles that make your drink fizzy. Carbon dioxide gas is added under pressure when the soda is bottled or canned. When you open the container, the air pressure in it drops and the gas is released, as it can no longer stay dissolved in the  soda. Warmer soda doesn't hold as much gas as cold soda, so if you want to keep that fizzy feeling, you need to drink your soda cold. Then when it warms up in your mouth, the bubbles will form.

Bubble Wars

Which bubbles are tougher: the bubbles in a bubble bath or the bubbles in shampoo? Let's see them fight it out. This is one project your parents will really appreciate!

WARNING: Some bubbles will die in the performance of this experiment.

You Will Need

- commercial bubble bath
- shampoo
- soap
- bathtub
- an adult helper

What to Do

1. Have an adult make you a huge, foaming bubble bath, using a commercial brand of bubble bath. Plop yourself in the bathtub.

2. Lather up some body soap on your hands and scoop up a handful of bubbles from the bath. What happened? Rinse off your hands in the tub.

3. Place a small dab of shampoo on your hands and work up a lather. Grab a handful of bubbles from the bath and see what happens.

What Happened

The chemicals used to make bubble bath, shampoo, and soap are different. The soap bubbles and shampoo bubbles will cause the bubble bath bubbles to burst as the different chemicals mix. Different manufacturers use different combinations of chemicals in their products. We can't say for sure what's in your bath products, but a quick look at the labels should give you some idea.

Antibubbles

despite their name, "antibubbles" aren't evil suds intent on destroying "good bubbles." An antibubble is probably something you've never thought of before. So what are these things and where do they come from?

WARNING: You will need patience and practice for this activity.

You Will Need

- water
- table salt
- food coloring
- corn syrup
- a large bowl or bucket
- a large wide-mouthed glass jar
- liquid dishwashing detergent such as Ivory, Palmolive, or Dawn
- a really clean empty plastic bottle with a thin nozzle (an old squeezable mustard or ketchup bottle will work)

What to Do

1. Fill the bucket or bowl with water and add several tablespoons of dishwashing detergent.

2. Pour a thin film of corn syrup in the bottom of the glass jar.

3. Fill the glass jar with liquid from the bucket in step 1 and scoop any bubbles from the top. Add some more water to the jar to fill it to the very top.

4. Fill the squeeze bottle with liquid from the bucket or bowl in step 1. Add a pinch of salt to the squeeze bottle and a drop of food coloring.

5. Hold the squeeze bottle at a 45-degree angle to the top of the liquid in the jar, and place the nozzle just above the surface of the water. Squeeze the solution from the bottle into the glass jar. Try to create a round "blob" of the colored solution on the surface of the liquid. You'll need lots of practice to get this right.

liquid is a sphere of liquid surrounded by a wall of air. Like a traditional bubble, an antibubble can float. Fine, it floats to the surface of a liquid very slowly, but it does float. When an antibubble pops, tiny air bubbles (that form the antibubble's skin) rise to the surface of the liquid. The skin of an antibubble has colors just like a regular bubble's but they are really difficult to see.

Another way you might see antibubbles is to shake a "wave" ornament (the kind with two different colored liquids inside). See if you can create antibubbles by giving one of these ornaments a good shake.

6. Squeeze your nozzle through this blob to make a long tube of liquid in the jar. Do this several times and you may begin to see antibubbles form. These bubbles will be colored, and will sink to the bottom of the jar.

7. The corn syrup will cushion the fall of the bubbles, and they should slowly begin to rise to the top of the jar.

What Happened

As you have seen, an antibubble is different from a "regular bubble;" in fact, it's just the reverse: an antibubble in

Insect In a Bubble

There is an insect that uses a bubble as a mode of transportation. It's the black fly (family Simuliidae), a species that is distributed widely throughout the world. The larvae and pupae of black flies live under water. As a black fly pupa gets ready to hatch, it becomes inflated with gas. When the pupal shell breaks open, it releases the bubble of gas, inside which the adult fly remains safe and dry. The bubble and its cargo then float to the surface, where the bubble pops, and the fly takes off to begin life as an adult.

Glossary

Air pressure—The amount of force that air exerts under given conditions

Angle—The shape made by two straight intersecting lines, or two planes meeting at a point. Angles can be measured in degrees.

Antibubble—A sphere of liquid surrounded by a thin layer of air inside another liquid

Carbon dioxide—The colorless, odorless gas that is given off when we breathe

Carpenter's level—A device used by builders to make things level; it uses a bubble inside a glass or plastic tube

Compression—A squeezing together

Density—The amount of mass in an object per unit of volume

Detergent—A chemical cleaning agent that removes dirt and oil, primarily by breaking down the surface tension in water so that it more easily dissolves solutions

Evaporation—The process in which a liquid changes into a gas

Film—A thin layer of something such as soap or water

Formula—A description of a chemical or mixture giving its parts and their amounts

Liquid—The state of matter which has a definite volume and an indefinite shape

Membrane—A thin, soft bendable layer of something

Molecule—The basic matter of all things, whether water, soap, or air

Particle—One of the minute objects that form matter: an electron, an atom, or a molecule

Petrochemical—A chemical distilled from petroleum or natural gas

Pressure—A force exerted by squeezing (or compression) or by pushing outward or against

Solution—A mixture which appears to be uniform throughout, usually a liquid

Surface area—The total dimensions of the outer face(s) of an object

Surface tension—A property of liquids where the outer surface tends to form the smallest area possible

Thin film interference—A phenomenon that occurs when light is bent through a thin film of liquid material

Vial—A small container for liquids, usually made of glass or plastic

Volume—A numerical figure indicating the amount of space something takes up

Index